Last One
Chosen

Last One Chosen

Dorothy Hamilton

Illustrated by
James L. Converse

HERALD PRESS
Scottdale, Pennsylvania
Kitchener, Ontario
1982

Library of Congress Cataloging in Publication Data

Hamilton, Dorothy, 1906-
    Last one chosen.

    Summary: Because of his lame leg, Scott is never
chosen in ball games, but he eventually realizes that
some other choices are more important.
    [1. Physically handicapped—Fiction] I. Converse,
James, ill.   II. Title.
PZ7.H18136Las   [Fic]   82-3150
ISBN 0-8361-3306-4 (pbk.)   AACR2

LAST ONE CHOSEN
Copyright © 1982 by Herald Press, Scottdale, Pa. 15683
    Published simultaneously in Canada by Herald Press,
    Kitchener, Ont. N2G 4M5
Library of Congress Catalog Card Number: 82-3150
International Standard Book Number: 0-8361-3306-4
Printed in the United States of America
Design by Alice B. Shetler

82 83 84 85 86 87 88 10 9 8 7 6 5 4 3 2 1

To
Scott,
Mark,
and our friend,
Alan
Garinger.

1

SCOTT moved back three steps before throwing the rubber ball at the fifth board from the corner of the barn. *I'm pretty good when I'm this far away. I hit that old knothole eight times out of twelve today.*

He limped across the straw littered floor and looked through the wide door, both left and right and then straight ahead to the house. *No one in sight.*

He threw and chased the ball until the afternoon train whistled for the Medford Crossing. He took the lid from a rusty milk can, dropped his ball and torn mitt into the can, and carefully set a coffee can of nails on top. *No need to let people know what I'm doing. They'd say it was no use. Lame kids don't get to play in little league—or anywhere else. That's what they'd say.*

Scott saw his mother come out the back door and walk toward the clothesline. *Sometimes I wish I could tell her what I do in the barn. Often she thinks I'm back at the pond or reading under the apple tree. What did she say when I left the house today? Oh, I remember, "Going to get a little sunshine?" That's how she put it. I didn't lie. I did get a little, going to the barn, and some came through the cracks between the boards in the barn. Not much, but a little. Nobody'd ever get sunburned from that much.*

Scott opened the back gate, and as he went up the walk he listened to his own steps. *I don't walk click-click or thump-thump like everyone else. It's more like a click and a shuffle, or a thump and a thud, with me.*

That's one good thing about having to sit around for a long time and not walking at all for more than a year. I learned a lot of words and paid attention to sounds. I noticed how the rain made little clicks on the window and how the vines brushing against the glass made soft whispers.

Scott aimed the ball at the knothole in the wall of the barn. "I'm getting pretty good at hitting it," he thought. "But lame kids don't get to play in little league—or anywhere else."

8

"Well now Scott Alan Hardesty! I didn't hear you come through the gate."

"I've learned how to keep the chains from banging—how to let the gate come shut a little at a time."

"Trying to slip up on me, huh?"

"No, I just don't like the sounds of the chains. They clank like that mystery show Bob Jo listens to on radio."

"You're almost like a poet," Scott's mother said, "With your feeling for sounds."

"Not for all sounds, Mom. Not all!"

"Well, anyway, what *are* you thinking about being when you grow up? Have you changed from last week?"

"No, I don't even remember what I thought then."

"Well, to tell you the truth, neither do I. And there's plenty of time, plenty of choices."

Not as many for me as for other kids, Scott thought. *There's no use to say it. Mom would get that sad look in her eyes—sort of misty, like she's crying without making tears.*

His mother sat the basket of clean clothes on the washer in the back porch and went ahead of him into the kitchen. "I brought the mail in while you were out," she said, "and there's a package. I saved it for you to open."

"Thanks. I wonder what's inside. Do you know?"

"I know what I hope is there."

10

As Scott reached for a small knife to slit the tough tape, he remembered the sunshine boxes people sent when he was hurt, waiting for the torn tendons in his leg to heal. Only they never did heal all the way. Not even after the operation—which only made them shorter.

He opened the thin box which had been wrapped with tape and brown paper. "Wow! It's just what I wanted—a denim jacket with grippers like Dad's! Hey, there are two."

"That's what I ordered," his mother said as she sat down on the chair across from him at the kitchen table. "One's lined for winter. One's for now, for the first of school. Try them to see if they fit—if the catalog people sent the right size."

Scott tried both jackets and walked around the kitchen table, wearing first one and then the other. "Thanks, Mom," he said. "Are these for my birthday or something?"

"No. I don't buy gifts three months ahead, unless they are for Christmas."

"These are just like Mark's."

"I know. I called Jenny Calpert to see where she bought Mark's jacket. I heard you tell him his was neat and tough, at least seven times."

"I think I'll call Mark and tell him. Is it okay if he can come over?"

"Certainly. And if Jenny's not busy ask her to come along."

Scott went to the hall and sat down on the seat

end of the telephone bench. He dialed and waited while he heard seven sets of two buzzes. Then after a click Mark said, "Hello."

"Hey! You sound out of breath."

"I am," Mark said. "I was up in the cherry tree."

"I thought you weren't supposed to play up there," Scott said.

"Well, I wasn't. Captain Midnight was. Then she got scared. Dumb cat."

Scott started to ask why his friend called a *her* cat a man's name. Then he remembered Mark saying girls get to be captain of a team sometimes. *But I know he didn't think of that till afterward. He's making excuses like I do when I say I don't like to play leapfrog and other active games.*

When Scott asked Mark if he could come for a visit Mark said, "I'm pretty sure I can. But I have to ask."

"My mom says your mom should come too."

"Okay! See you soon."

As Scott went out on the front porch to wait, he thought, *It's like always. When I'm just with Mom or excited about things I don't notice my limp. It's not that way at school, except when Mark's the only one that can hear or see me hippity-hoppiting around.*

A car came around the bend in the road. At first Scott thought it was going to come up the drive. *I guess it was going slow because of the crooked place in the road. It looks something like Dr. White's car. But he might have traded for a new one by now.*

He shook his head. *Thinking about the doctor makes me afraid again. I'm afraid both Mom and Dad will decide to try that new kind of operation—that they'll decide the same thing. But so far Dad hasn't changed his mind.*

He heard the ring of the bell on Mark's bike before it came within sight. *He's going too fast,* Scott thought. *He'll ram into the gatepost.* But as he watched, the bike slipped past the square post and coasted across the short grass in the barnlot.

"Some day you're going to end up wrapped around that big old chunk of wood," Scott warned.

"Think so?" Mark said as he jumped over the low wire fence and sat down on the edge of the porch.

"Yeah. You're always taking chances—doing things I don't dare to try."

"Could be that's 'cause you're smarter than I am," Mark said.

"You're always saying that."

" 'Cause it's true."

"But don't act like you feel bad about me being smarter—if it's true," Scott said.

"It's true all right," Mark said. "No one's good at everything."

"Like I'm not good at games. How come you never say anything about what I can't do?"

"That's easy. I don't think about that part," Mark said. "Besides it's like I said. No one's good at everything."

Scott's mother came to the door and talked through the screen wire. "Jenny not coming?"

"Oh, I forgot. She will as soon as she takes something out of the oven. I can't tell what. It's a surprise!"

The sun was a shining orange ball that seemed to touch the top of trees on the rim of the earth.

"You glad school's about to start?" Mark asked.

Scott nodded. "Mostly, except for gym."

"That's the best part for me."

"I know." Scott thought about telling his friend that he'd been pitching balls at a knothole every-day—even on Sunday when Dad and Mom take naps or watch TV and when no one comes.

"Does it hurt? Your leg I mean, when you run and jump."

"No, not now. It's just that I'm slow." Then before he could think about deciding not to tell Mark what he'd been doing he heard himself say, "I'm not bad at one thing though."

"You mean lessons, and tropical fish, and things like that?"

"No, not any of that. At hitting a knothole with a rubber ball."

"Are you kidding?"

"No, I've been practicing. Want to see me do it?"

"I sure do. Where?"

14

"Come on. But don't tell anyone. I didn't mean to open my big mouth."

"But you did. Man! You know what! We could play pass. You wouldn't have to run much."

"I'd like that. It wouldn't be like being the slowest person on a team."

2

SCOTT reached into the rusty milk can, handed the mitt and ball to Mark, and led the way to the level place back of the barn. "I do better where there are no bumps. I don't stumble as much," he explained.

They'd thrown the ball back and forth several times when Mark said, "Man you throw hard. I've missed some of them because of your speed. And those I caught stung my hand. You're some pitcher."

"But not like a real one. I mean that old knothole stands still. It's not like a batter leaning over the plate."

"Yes, but you get the ball where you want it. That's control."

16

"It is?"

"It sure is. I'm going to bring a bat the next time I come, and a regulation ball. I've got extras."

"Well, I don't know why. I mean—"

"To have fun, for one thing. This is great."

The boys played until the shadows grew long and they were tired. After they put the ball and mitt in the can and left the barn Scott's father came home. The red and white pickup truck stopped a few feet from them. "What you two up to?" John Hardesty said. "Making caves in the bales of hay again."

"Not this time," Scott said. "We better get washed up for supper."

"I'd better be getting home."

"No, you're to stay," Scott's father said. "I got the news at the elevator. My wife left word that I was to stop for a half gallon of ice cream because the Calperts were eating with us."

"Not all of us," Mark said. "Dad's on his long run to someplace in Missouri."

"Well, two Calperts are better than none. That's what I always say."

"Dad!" Scott said. "I never heard you say that."

"Yes you did! Just now."

Scott felt good when his father was in a teasing mood. Sometimes he wasn't. He hadn't been when Dr. White told them about the new way of repairing damaged tendons, of making them longer or stretching them, or whatever. *I think it makes him remember the day when the big mower whipped around and caught the back of my leg. He remembers he was driving the tractor.*

Scott shook his head as he followed Mark through the gate. *I don't want to think about that anymore. I don't as much as I did. I wonder if Dad still does?*

Jenny Calpert was at the back door. "I was coming to call you, to let you know I'm here."

"No need," John Hardesty said. "My stomach knows it's time to eat. It told me an hour or so ago, before I had the truck half loaded with calf pellets. But that's the life of a farmer—seeing to it that livestock have feed before stoking his own furnaces."

"You aren't exactly undernourished," Scott's mother said.

The grown-ups talked to each other most of the time. Scott wished he'd asked Mark not to tell about his knothole target. *I don't know why I don't want Mom and Dad to know, but I don't.*

After the meal the boys went to Scott's room. "I haven't seen your fish for a long time," Mark said. "Bought any new ones?"

"No, but I have some new ones. The live-bearers had babies—the fancy guppies and the black mollies."

After the meal the boys went to Scott's room. "I haven't seen your fish for a long time," Mark said. "Have you bought any new ones?"

"They must be really little."

"They are. I have to look a long time and know where to look."

"What do you mean *where*?"

"Well, the guppies hide in the grass-like strip which floats on top of the aquarium. The Mollies dig down in the gravel."

"Hide? Why?"

"Because the big fish might eat them," Scott explained. "Some are sort of mean. But I don't have the worst kind—like angelfish."

"That doesn't make sense—that angelfish could be mean."

"Well, they are," Scott said. "They're pretty but fierce. I don't want any fish that aren't friendly."

"It's too bad some people are like that," Mark said.

"It sure is. People like—"

"I know who you're thinking about—Raymie Darter. Man, he's *mean* all right."

The boys watched the fish dart behind and around the plastic plants and past the curved seashells. "The guppies are my favorites," Scott said. "Their tails wave back and forth like fans."

"The red ones are nice," Mark said. "What did you call them?"

"Wagtail swords. Sometimes I don't like to clean the filters and add water. But I don't want to give up my aquarium. Not yet anyway."

"I gave up on a couple things like hamsters and

20

rock collecting so far," Mark said.

"My Mom says that's the way we find out what's important."

"Could be," Mark agreed. "Say someone's coming. Might be time to go home. Hey, I was thinking. Wouldn't it be easier if you had a room downstairs?"

"I did, remember? When I couldn't walk at all. But this is better."

"Are you sure you won't let us take you home?" Scott's mother was saying as she and Jenny Calpert came into the room.

"No, I can ride Mark on the bike if he holds his legs out straight."

"You're not afraid to walk into your house after dark?"

"No, not with Butch around. His bark and pushed-up nose would scare most prowlers away. They don't know that his English bulldog face is more frightening than he is—fortunately for us."

"See you Friday if not before," Mark said as he waited for his mother to get set on the bike.

"Right. I wonder if the bus will pick you up first this year?"

"I forget how it was last semester," Mark said. "Whichever, it'll be the other way around this time."

Scott felt lonely after the bike moved beyond the circle of light from the barnlot lamp post.

"You going to your room?" Scott's father asked.

"Why? It's not late."

"No, but Sam Darter's coming by to look at the planter I'm selling."

"Wow," Scott said. "Do you think Raymie will be with him?"

"Probably. He usually is. Doesn't that kid have any friends?"

Scott shrugged his shoulders. "Not here."

"You never told me why he's bad news to you. Even when I asked, you didn't give much of an answer. Why?"

"Oh, Dad, you'd get mad. And you have to work with Raymie's dad sometimes."

"If there's a reason why I'd get riled up maybe I *should* know."

Scott went to the sink and filled a paper cup with water after rinsing it three times. He took three swallows and turned to face his father. "It's because he calls me names."

"What kind of names?"

"Like about being lame. Leadfoot and Dragdog. *See*, Dad, you're already mad. Your ears are red."

"It seems to me that kind of thing would have ended by now," Scott's mother said.

"It has with everyone else. But Runoff Raymie never shuts up. That's what Mark calls him, 'cause he keeps jabbering on and on."

"I suppose that's name calling too," Scott's mother said.

"There's a difference," John Hardesty

answered. "Raymie gets labeled for what he does. But he calls you names for something that's not your fault."

Dad agrees Raymie talks too much, Scott thought.

"Well, I'll not let him come inside," Dad said. "I'll waylay them outside the house."

"What will you say, Dad?"

"That you're in bed? No, that won't do. And I won't lie and say you're not here. Why beat about the bush? I'll say I don't think you like to be called names. Okay?"

"Well, it's the truth. He does it in front of everyone, even in class if the teacher is far enough away."

"So! It's time to put an end to that."

As Scott chose an apple from the wooden bowl he thought, *I wonder what Old Run—Raymie will do next. Probably more of the same. He seems to be stuck in some kind of rut, like a needle on a record player.*

3

THE THREE MEMBERS of the Hardesty family watched television until a wide path of light swept across the family room. "That's Darter's truck," Scott's father said. "I can tell by the muffler that doesn't muffle much."

Scott thought of peeking to see if Raymie came along but decided he didn't want to take a chance of being seen. "If old Raymie gets the idea of coming in he'll find a way. He's sneaky."

"I think I'll go to the basement," Liz Hardesty said. "I'm going to sort through some boxes, and see what's worth donating to the rummage sale. Want to come along, Scott? Perhaps you'll find some of your old games or toys you can bear to give away."

24

"Mom! Every year we do this and mostly we decide to keep what we have."

"I know. I give away less than we accumulate. That's why there are twice as many boxes as there were when we moved into this house."

"Sometimes it's hard for me to remember when we lived in the little house," Scott said. "I can remember a lot more about when Gram and Granddad lived here."

"It could be there's a reason. We tend to recall the pleasanter times—thank heavens! And you were hurt at the other place. Here are two empty cartons. I'll put discards in one. Yoy may be able to fill the other one part way."

Scott looked through one box, stopping to glance through two fishing magazines and to whirl the metal arrow which was part of a baseball game. "I played with this a lot when I was hurt—when Mark came. I'll keep it." He sorted out five paperback books, a top that still hummed when it was wound, and two maze games with ball bearings that rolled where they should if he was careful long enough.

"Do you think about that time a lot?" Scott's mother asked as she refolded a striped bedspread.

"When I was hurt? Some, but not as much as I used to. Except when I think about maybe needing another operation."

"Does that make you afraid?"

"I guess so. If I was sure it'd work, I wouldn't

care that much about the pain. But I'd still be scared."

"I know. Dad and I feel that way too."

"You think we'll do it?" Scott asked.

"I don't know. But this one thing I can say. It won't be done against anyone's will—not yours, mine, or your father's. You don't need to think we're going to leave you out of this decision."

"I didn't, Mom."

"Good—we'll have to—Listen. Was that the phone? Yes."

Scott stacked the books and games he was keeping and shoved that box back into the closet. He was starting up the stairs when his mother came to the half-way landing. "Mark's waiting to talk to you. You're going to be surprised."

"What's up?" Scott asked as he reached the telephone.

"Your Mom didn't tell you, huh? Well, I'm going to stay at your house for four days. Okay?"

"Sure. What's going on? Are your folks taking a vacation or something?"

"In a way. Dad called and said he picked up a load and is going on to Pennsylvania. Mom's to meet him in Richmond along U.S. 70."

"Don't you wish you could go along?"

"No. I did last summer. Anyway, I'd rather be here when school starts. I really mean when softball practice begins."

"Man, this is great. I might think of something for you to bring."

26

"I've already made a list. Call me if you think of stuff."

"Okay. See you."

"Is that good news?" Scott's mother asked.

"It sure is."

"Let's think about where you can sleep. Would you rather move the folding cot into your room, sleep in the guest room, or—"

"Mom! You know where I'd like to sleep. In the lighthouse."

"I was afraid of that."

"You mean you don't want us to sleep in the room at the top of the house?"

"No, I wouldn't say that. I can see how sleeping up there would be a lot of fun. I've thought of doing it myself."

"You could. I'd stay with you, if you want. But why did you say you were *afraid*?"

"Because we have work to do. Cobwebs to sweep away. A floor to be swept. Cots to be carried."

"If it's too much—"

"No, no. Come on. Get your flashlight and Dad's electric lantern. I do wish your granddad had put wiring up there."

"Let me go ahead," Scott's mother said as they went to the wide hall and started up the winding staircase. "Otherwise you'll get poked by the handles of the broom and dust mop."

The way was lighted to the second floor. Scott waited while his mother unhooked the square section of the ceiling of the upper floor, moved it back, and pulled down the short ladder. "Think you can make this?"

"Sure, if you'll reach back for one of these lights."

When Scott pulled himself up to the small square room he could see the moon through one window.

"It's really beautiful—the world I mean," Scott's mother said as she walked to each of the four windows. "The lights in the houses look like fireflies that are standing still and those of the cars over on State Road 35 are like a twinkling bracelet."

"I used to play here a lot before I was hurt."

"Since then I've been afraid you'd fall."

"I know."

"Well, I've learned to be less anxious, less protective, because you do so well. But I'm going to check at night to be sure you boys have that trapdoor in place. Otherwise I'll be lying awake thinking you might roll out of bed, and tumble all the way down to the second floor."

"Some bump that would be," Scott said with a chuckle.

As Scott brushed at cobwebs he thought about what they'd bring to the lighthouse. *I'll take my transistor and extra batteries and something to eat and drink. Maybe Mark will have something—like his record player that either plugs in or runs on batteries. I'll call him later.*

"Will Dad help move the cots up tonight?" Scott asked.

"We'll see."

That means she's not sure if he will or not, Scott thought.

"Here, hold this dust pan for me, please," Scott's mother said. "After I dump this litter we'll be ready to go down. I'm going to let the mop and broom slide down by themselves. There's nothing on them to break."

The wooden handles bumped against the ladder. Then Scott heard his father say, "What's going on up there? I already know what's coming down. I nearly got whacked."

After Scott explained that he and Mark were going to sleep in the lighthouse he asked, "Do you have time to bring cots up? Or would tomorrow be better?"

"Tonight's as good a time as any."

After the beds were placed under the east and west windows, Liz Hardesty made another trip down to the second floor for pillows, blankets, and sheets. While she made up the second cot, Scott and his father sat on the first. "I've had some mighty good times up here myself."

"You slept here?" Scott asked.

"I did. Sometimes alone. Sometimes with my cousin Bob. I liked it best alone. I could pretend."

"Like what, Dad?"

"That this was a real lighthouse and that the fields were the ocean. And when a freight train came over on the C & O tracks, it was a ship I was warning away from the rocks."

"Dad," Scott said. "Do you want to sleep up here with me tonight maybe?"

"But Scott," his mother said. "You'll be up here for three nights after this with Mark."

"But that's not the same. That's not like being with Dad."

His father put an arm around his shoulders and said, "Then let's get ready for bed. It's time to—"

"I know," Scott said. "It's time to end this day so we can get ready for the next."

4

AT FIRST Scott didn't know where he was when he opened his eyes the next morning. He blinked and stretched before realizing he was in the lighthouse. By turning his head and raising up a little he could see out the east window. *It's beginning to be day. The sky's a little rosy above the trees. It's probably rosy below them, too, only I can't see back there.*

As he lay back he thought of something he'd heard about sound, that if someone shot a gun and no one was near enough to hear there'd be no sound. *That's hard for me to understand. If no one sees the sky is it still rosy?*

"You awake?" his father asked as the cot frame creaked with his moving.

"Yes, part way."

"We'd probably be wise to get up. I have to sow wheat today. It's that time of year."

"Dad, why did the people who built this house want a room like this?"

"Hard to tell. My Dad said they probably copied it from someone else who built this type house."

"But why would the person they copied after want one?" Scott asked.

"I've thought about *that*. They couldn't have needed the extra space in a house this size. And heating way up here before my father tore out part of the winding staircase and boxed this off must have taken a lot of fuel."

"I guess people didn't always worry about saving energy," Scott said.

"No, not here. When gas was first discovered, they had flames going from an up-ended pipe day and night. But back to your first question. I've wondered if some settler wasn't homesick for the east, for the sea."

"And built a place where he could see farther?"

"Could be. But we'll probably never know for sure. These old walls don't talk."

"If they did it'd sure be spooky," Scott said. "I might not want to sleep up here."

Scott had asked three times what time his mother thought Mark would be coming, before breakfast was over. "Didn't he say? Or his Mom?"

"Not exactly. Only that Jenny is to be at the

truck stop by eleven. How long will it take her to get there?"

"Less than an hour."

"Couldn't I call?"

"Mark is probably busy. Don't they have animals to feed?"

"Not hamsters. But he has Silver his pony and Mrs. Calpert's Siamese cats. Who will feed them and Butch while Mark is here?"

"They'll have that all worked out. And *we* have things to do," Scott's mother said. "Like cooking and making chocolate-bit cookies and—well, I'm sure there are other jobs—beyond the two telephone poles."

As Scott sifted brown sugar over his steaming oatmeal he thought. *Some people would think Mom is kooky if they heard her talking about telephone poles. She just means she doesn't see what to do too far ahead. Like the morning when it was foggy and she worried about missing the bend in the road and running into the fence. But she could see two telephone poles ahead then too.*

"I'll be at the back of the farm until time to eat again," Scott's father said as he pushed his chair from the table. "If you and Mark want to come back be sure to fasten the chain on the gate. Otherwise we'll have Black Angus cattle in the wrong places."

"We'd go the long way around," Scott said. "Mark's afraid of cows. He says their big old eyes scare him."

"I didn't think he'd be—but I suppose everyone's afraid of something."

Scott had fed his fish, added water to the aquarium, and taken table scraps outside to the chickens before Mark came circling into the backyard.

"I thought you'd bring some things along," Scott said as he went to the fence.

"I did. My bike. Mom's coming in the car with some clothes and the record player. And the bat and balls. I didn't forget them."

Scott didn't say what he was thinking, that he was not ready to let others know he was trying to get better at playing ball. *What they don't know they can't say smart stuff about. And some would.*

When Jenny Calpert unlocked the trunk of the car Mark asked, "Where shall we put my stuff? Upstairs?"

"Yes," Scott said. "A long way up the stairs if it's okay. I'll explain later."

"Now you be careful" Mark's mother said as she walked to the front of the car. "Don't go climbing trees or cause Scott and his folks any trouble."

"I *won't*, Mom."

"He won't," Scott's mother said.

"Well, I'll call tomorrow night just to be sure. Check Markie, see if you have your book rental money and the back door key."

"I've checked four times. See! Goodbye Mom."

"She acts like she's going to be away for a year," Mark said.

"That's how we feel when we leave you," Liz Hardesty said as she patted Mark's cheek.

That's true, Scott thought. *Every time she left me at the hospital she acted like that. I remember. So did Dad.*

"What are we going to do first?" Mark asked as he lifted his record player from the end of the walk.

"We'll go to my room. And I'll tell you where we will sleep, I hope—if it's okay with you."

"Well—*tell* me."

Before Scott finished explaining about the lighthouse Mark said, "Come on, show me. How come I never saw this place before now?"

"I don't know. I never thought to show you, I guess. We've only lived here a year or a little more."

"I know since your Grandpa and Grandma moved to town."

"Mom," Scott called. "We're going to the lighthouse."

"Be careful."

"I knew she'd say that."

"So does mine. All the time."

"Wow," Mark said as he looked around. "This is really a super place. Look! I can see clear to the end of Prairie Creek Reservoir, as far as the dam."

"I know. That's because we're up above everything that g s in our way. Dad and I slept here last night. He talked about when he was growing up."

"Well," Mark said, "I don't ever remember wishing it was time to go to bed—not in my whole life. But I won't be mad tonight."

"The only bad thing is that going up and down isn't easy," Scott said. "We'll have to do what has to be done ahead of time—like bringing up some food and something to drink. What do you want to do now?"

"Well, if it's okay, I'd like to see how good you are at hitting a bat. That's bigger than a knothole."

"But not as big as the side of the barn."

"Come on. I'll get the things out of the canvas bag."

As the boys crossed the barn lot a truck came around the bend. "That sounds like the truck Raymie's dad drives," Scott said. "Is it coming here?" He wished the balls and bat would disappear, or that he could crawl into a hole somewhere. *But it's no use wishing. It's him and old Raymie—*

"Your pa home?" Mr. Darter asked after he shut off the unmuffled motor.

"Back in the field."

"Tell him one planter plate cracked. That wasn't part of the deal."

"Okay."

"What you guys doin'?" Raymie asked.

"Oh, nothing much. Just fooling around."

"Looks to me like you're getting ready to play ball. If you want someone to play with you, Mark, I could—"

"I got someone," Mark said. "Don't miss out on anything on account of us."

"Oh yeah?" Raymie said.

"Yeah. See you."

"Wow," Scott said. "I was scared he was going to climb right out of that truck."

"He might have last week."

"Why then? Why not now?"

"Oh, he was saying a bunch of dumb stuff and I scared him into shutting up. I know some things he's done—like painting Mr. Stafford's front door black."

"Looks like he'd be the one to scare you into not telling," Scott said.

"Sometimes it works that way. But Raymie scares easy. Come on. Let's play ball."

As they went around the barn Scott thought, *I'll bet Raymie was saying dumb stuff about me and Mark stood up to him—for me.*

5

"FIRST *you* pitch," Mark said as they walked across the grass. "I want to see if I can hit you."

"The way I've been doing it is to try to hit the knothole."

"Don't think that way. Just try to make the ball go where you want it to go."

"I'll try."

Mark hit the first three pitches. Scott wished he could throw some strikes that Mark would miss. Then something happened inside his mind. He got a feeling about the ball, about where he could make it go. After Mark missed a dozen times Scott asked, "Hey, you trying to miss or something to make me feel good?"

"No, I wouldn't cheat on you like that. I can't

38

tell how that ball's going to curve or if it is. Now you try hitting. I'll do the chasing if you want."

Scott took a deep breath as he held the bat back over his shoulder. *I wish my heart wasn't beating so fast. Why is it? Maybe 'cause he wants me to be good, so we could be better friends, or something like that.*

"Ready?" Mark asked.

"I guess."

Scott missed four balls in a row and again he wanted to quit. *But that would be dumb. To give up before I really try. I'll just have to keep my eye on that old ball.* He shrugged his shoulders and watched Mark draw back. *I know where that ball's going. I've watched them come at me from the side of the barn on that kind of a line.* He changed his position, then swung under the ball and lifted into a high arc.

"Run, man, run," Scott said. He was jumping up and down.

Scott glanced up. The ball was headed over the snowball bush and over the back fence. He'd rounded all the bases before Mark yelled, "Wow, you hit that one out of the ball park. It sounded like you cracked the bat."

Scott shook his head. "I don't know what happened."

"You connected, that's what!"

"Well, I guess if you hit the ball far enough you can get around the bases, no matter how slow you are at running."

"Are you ready to quit for awhile?"

"If you are. We'll probably be called to eat before long—when Dad comes up, for sure. We could get our hands scrubbed ahead of time."

As Mark slushed water over his face Scott thought, *I hope he's not getting the idea that I can play with the kids at school. It'd not be the same as here—even if someone did choose me.*

At the table Mark told about the long ball Scott had hit. "Pitching at a knothole was good practice."

Scott glanced sideways at his parents. *They don't look surprised. They aren't asking any questions. Maybe they didn't hear what Mark said.*

"Do you have something planned for this afternoon?" Liz Hardesty asked. She spooned fresh fruit into small glass bowls and went on talking. "If you don't, or even if you do, I'm thinking about going in to the shopping center. Anyone want to hitch a ride?"

Scott looked at Mark who shook his head.

"Me neither," Scott said, "Could we go to the woods—ride back with Dad?"

"In the wagon, but not on the tractor," John Hardesty said. "There aren't enough hand-holds on the tractor for two passengers. But remember, I'll not be coming up until nearly sundown."

"We can walk," Scott said, "if we get ready before you."

"I'm glad we're going to the woods," Mark said.

"I never have been that far back except the day I went hunting with my dad. I was scared the whole time he'd find something to shoot."

"I've been hunting a lot of times with Granddad," Scott said.

The boys sat on top of the sacks of seed wheat. They said "ah" as they bounced over the rough ground, laughing at how their voices vibrated. "Here, take your thermos of lemonade and a share of the sugar cookies," John Hardesty said. "And let me know if you decide to go to the house ahead of me."

"It's going to be hard to get into the woods," Scott said. "The grass is tall and there are wild blackberry bushes along this side."

"Why isn't the grass tall farther on?"

"Because it's shady there and things don't grow as fast—except for some wild flowers and saplings."

"What's a sapling?"

"A little tree."

"This is like a roof," Mark said as they walked into the shadowed forest, "a roof with a green ceiling."

"There's a place over there that's the best part for me," Scott said. "We used to come a lot, Grandad and me. He'd tell me tales of olden times while I swung in the saddle of the wild grapevine."

"Saddle of a vine?"

"That's what we called it. Come on. It's easier

to *show* you." Scott led the way to a slope that led down across a space the width of a room and then up again. Two trees stood near either side and they were connected by two ropes of thick vines.

"How did they grow that way across that space?" Mark asked.

"Grandad doesn't think they did, not all by themselves. He *figures*—that's what he says, for *think*—that someone trained them. Maybe an Indian."

"Wow! Do you think that's true?"

"I like to think about it. These trees are big and old and could have been here that long ago."

"This is sure scratchy," Mark said as he ran his hand back and forth along one rope of the grapevine swing.

"That's why we have the saddle." Scott went to a tree a few feet away. "See this is hollow on one side." He pulled and dragged a dark brown bundle to where Mark waited. "There's an old blanket inside, in this old sheepskin coat. That's why it doesn't get wet, at least not very wet." He unbuckled two straps and spread the five layers of material over the center of the swaying vines. He wrapped the straps around either end and pulled them tight before fastening the buckles. "There! Try it."

Two trees were connected by two ropes of thick vines. "Granddad figures someone trained the vines to grow that way. Maybe an Indian."

Mark jumped up and mounted the blanket saddle. "It isn't hard, not like I thought it would be. It sort of swings by itself."

"I know. Sometimes it almost puts you to sleep."

After Scott and Mark had each taken two turns on the swing, the boys stretched out on their stomachs with their heads at the top of a slope. "You can hear a lot of little sounds here, can't you?" Mark said.

"Yeah. Crickets, and squirrels running in the leaves, and frogs over in the pond. I've seen toads, all lumpy and brown, hopping around here. It's like they're on springs. But the best things were the deer. They still are."

"You mean they're around here now?" Mark said.

"Sure, I've seen them twice this summer. Evening's the best time. They come to our pasture to drink in the creek."

"Man, I'd sure like to see that."

"We'll ask Dad. If he has time he'll come back with us. He does with me. We hide at the edge of the creek up that way, in the cattails."

"I never did take this much time just to be still and listen," Mark said. "I'm always on the go. You said your grandpa told stories. What kind?"

"About around here. Some he remembered. Some he'd heard—like how people used to drive turkeys, big bunches of them, through here to Cincinnati."

44

"Why?"

"To sell them."

"Looks like it'd be hard to keep them from getting lost," Mark said.

"I guess they had a lot of men doing it. At night, they'd sleep in the trees—the turkeys I mean."

"Tell some more." Mark turned over and crooked one arm over his eyes.

Scott told about the time when people thought oil was under the ground and came from far away to drill for it. "My Grandpa knew a man who came all the way from Scotland. They didn't find much oil, but that's when they found natural gas. Grandpa still says that if we had only a part of what people wasted in the early days we wouldn't be so worried about energy."

"I never heard any of this," Mark said. "It's sort of weird swinging on a vine where Indians could have sat. And being where oil wells were drilled makes the world seem different."

"I like to imagine how it was more than how it will be."

"You mean like how it will be in outer space living on the moon."

"Yeah, the TV shows where people go way out to other planets are not my favorite kind. People here are okay with me, mostly anyway."

"Except for Run-on-Raymie, huh?"

"Yeah."

6

"THERE'S THE evening train," Scott said as he watched a cardinal hop along a twig of the walnut tree at the top of the ridge."

"How'd you know? I mean does it go the same time every day?"

"Except on Sundays."

"I never noticed," Mark said.

"That's because, like you said, you're always on the go. You've never had to sit all day—for a lot of days."

"Do you ever talk about what happened the day you got hurt?"

"Didn't anyone tell you? A mower blade caught the back of my leg when the tractor turned."

"I know *that*. But—"

46

"But you want to know why I didn't get out of the way."

"Well, yes. It seems like you would."

"I know, but my dog was with me. Dad shouted, 'Hold onto his collar so his legs won't get cut off!' I did but the crazy dog saw a rabbit or something. He lunged and the collar slipped off right over his head. I didn't think about Dad turning at the end of the field. I tried to catch Sport, and the very end of the blade whipped around and caught the back of my leg. The doctors said if the tooth on the mower hadn't been bent—it would have been worse."

Mark turned over, put his head on his folded arms and rolled it back and forth. "It hurts me to think about it."

"Well, it does me too. But the real pain was worse. That's why I don't know if I want to be operated on again."

"Would that help?"

"Maybe. The doctors know more about what can be done now than when I was hurt. At least those who worked on me do. There's something to do for tendons that were all torn up. That's what makes my leg shorter. Maybe they can slit what's there and stretch the stuff."

"You mean it'd be like new?"

"I don't think so, not all the way, because it's been awhile. But they think they could fix it so I wouldn't limp so much—drag a dog, as Raymie said."

"Do you think you will be operated on?"

"I don't know. Mom says I can help decide."

"I don't know how I'd feel in your place."

"Do you want me to walk better?" Scott asked. "Would that make a difference to you?"

Mark sat up and gave Scott a little slap on his back. "That's dumb! I don't think about how you walk. How you feel is more important to me."

"I can't keep from thinking about going back to the hospital," Scott said. "I mean, I'm doing okay now. Oh, let's do something."

"We could ride on the tractor."

"Dad wouldn't let us. He's scared of someone getting hurt. He almost quit being a farmer after the accident. That's what Mom said. But people get hurt lots of places. Well, we could go to the house. Mom's home."

"How do you know that? You can't see the house from here."

"I heard the dinner bell. Two dings. That's the signal."

The boys crossed into the pasture and waited at the corner of the section of the field where Scott's father was sowing wheat. When he saw them he stood up and waved. "That's another signal, I guess," Mark said.

"I almost forgot," Mark said as they walked through the gate into the yard. "I'm supposed to go home a time or two to get the mail from our box and feed the animals. Want to go along? I can ride you on my bike."

"I might go with you tomorrow."

"Okay. Check with your Mom."

The boys waited for Scott's father. They went into the house together and found supper waiting. As Scott spread butter over his pecan waffle he said, "Mr. Darter was here, Dad. He said he didn't get something that belonged to the planter."

"He'll be back. You can count on that. He doesn't give up on getting all that's coming to him. Or all that he thinks he has coming."

"How soon are we going up to the lighthouse?" Mark asked as they left the table.

"It's too early. Besides there's no TV up there. There aren't even any electric lights or plug-in places."

Before the first half hour television show was over Scott heard someone talking in a loud voice in the kitchen.

"No matter, Mrs. Hardesty. I'll go on in. This has to be straightened out."

"Wow!" Scott whispered. "Mr. Darter is here, and probably Raymie." He sat up on his end of the couch and he and Mark both spread their legs toward the middle. *I guess neither one of us wants to leave room for Raymie*, he thought.

"I came to get what's owed to me," Mr. Darter said, as he set his wide straw hat farther back on his head. Raymie walked in with his father.

"I heard you were here," John Hardesty said. "Come out. I'll find the plates."

Raymie sat down and said, "I'd as soon wait here with these guys."

"Suit yourself," his father said. "But come on the run when I toot. Hear!"

"Have you been having a lot of fun?" Raymie asked.

Scott wanted to pretend he hadn't heard. He looked straight at the TV but didn't have his mind on the program.

Mark pushed on Scott's foot with one of his. "Yeah."

"What'd you do?"

"Oh, lots of things," Mark said.

"I reckon you didn't play ball long. Couldn't have been much fun. Right?"

"Why would you think a thing like that?" Mark asked.

"On account of him. Being like *that.*"

Mark swung his legs to the floor. "You're about as wrong as you can be. You'd really be surprised if—but there's no use to tell you."

"Tell me what?"

"Hey, your Dad's honking. See you," Mark said.

After Raymie left Scott said, "Don't you get tired of standing up for me?"

"I didn't know I was doing that. It's just standing up to Raymie. I been doing that for as long as I can remember."

"How do you mean?"

"Oh that guy's always putting someone down.

50

Sammy because he's black and Larry because his grandmother makes his pants and girls just because that's what they are, girls. And teachers because that's what *they* are."

"I think we could begin to gather up our things and get ready for bed," Scott said. "Probably we won't get out of taking baths."

"I heard that," Scott's mother said from the door. "You won't. When you're finished, I have a box of snacks ready—apples and chunks of cheese and cookies. There's warm chocolate milk in this thermos."

The clock chimed 9:30 before they were ready to climb the ladder.

"I wish there was a way of communicating," Liz Hardesty said as she waited at the foot. "I might not hear you if you need me."

"Oh, Mom. We can yell. There's a crack around that door. Besides we can open it from up here, too, with rope."

"I know, but be careful."

"The big flashlight makes this square room so light we could read if we wanted," Scott said.

"Do you?"

"No, not tonight. But I did bring up some books."

They turned the knob of the radio to low and talked above it. Mark sat on the end of his cot and looked out the window. "This is a real neat hideout, only no one's hunting us. This would be a good place to get away from Raymie."

"It sure would," Scott said. "You're going to think I'm dumb or crazy, but sometimes I feel a little sorry for Raymie."

"That *is* a little dumb. Why, he's just a big old clunk."

"I know. But don't you think he knows how we all feel? That we don't want him around?"

"I don't know. I never thought about that."

"I have, a little anyway. Most of the time I wish I was someplace else."

"Wow," Mark said. "I never thought I'd feel even a little bit sorry for the guy. But maybe he could change, and not always be putting everyone down."

"Maybe," Scott said. "Ready to put out the light?"

"First could I try something? Let me take the flashlight and shine it from each of the windows. Someone might think it's a signal. Think so?"

"If anyone is paying attention, they might."

"Before we go to bed, I want to shine the flashlight from each of the windows. Someone might think it's a signal? Think so?"

7

SCOTT was all the way awake the next morning before he realized he hadn't been dreaming. There was a noise but it wasn't a train rumbling. It was thunder. He turned over and looked up at the window. *It's partly daylight,* he thought. A flash of lightning zigzagged across the gray-blue sky. He looked over at Mark's cot. *I guess he's not awake.*

He raised up on one elbow and tried to imagine how it would be to live in a real lighthouse. *If water was all around and beating on the rocks outside it might not be so great. But that's when I'd be in one, during a bad storm. That's when ships would be in the most danger.*

A mist of rain came through the half-opened

window. He carefully pulled down on the wood frame and lay back and watched the glass get showered. *I wonder what we'll do all day? Mark could be really bored being stuck inside.*

"I heard you," Mark said.

"Heard me what?"

"Shut the window. You sure do hear the rain plain up here."

"I know. It's coming on four windows all close to us."

"And the wind. People in lighthouses probably hear it like this all the time. I might not like living in one if it stormed."

"I know. But that's why they were there, partly anyway. To warn sailors of dangerous rocks in bad weather."

"I guess we won't be playing ball today," Mark said.

"In the barn we could," Scott said. "But that might not be as much fun for you. To tell you the truth I don't know if it was all that great for me. I just wanted to be better—to see if I could ever play ball again."

"We could make tunnels with the bales of hay, like your dad said."

"It wouldn't be easy. There's so much hay up there we couldn't make many tunnels. There's not that much room. But we could try. Let's get up. Okay?"

Before Scott finished lacing his sneakers he heard a creaking from the trap door. "Mom's letting the ladder down. Grab your jeans or they'll go tumbling down."

During breakfast Scott's father and mother talked about what they could do during this rainy day. "I can't sow wheat or do any other outdoor job. Any ideas?"

"I have a few," Liz Hardesty said. "Like making shelves in the utility room, and putting new tile for those that split in the bathroom, and—"

"I don't think Dad likes those ideas, Mom," Scott said.

"Well, who said I thought he would? But this one he might. And you too, both of you. I thought we might go to Metamora."

"Wow, Mom, that's a super idea. Right, Mark?"

"I don't know. What's there?"

"Oh, an old town on an old canal. And a boat that's pulled by horses walking along the side. And a museum. And a root beer cellar. Lots of stuff."

"It might be raining there," Scott's father said.

"So what? As my mother used to say, we're neither sugar nor salt nor no one's honey. We won't melt."

"Does that make sense to you?" Mark whispered.

"A little. But I've heard it before. I've had time to think about it."

"Now that I've pondered the matter for two whole minutes," John Hardesty said, "it might be an advantage for me to go in that direction. I need to get some parts in New Castle for the combine."

"Okay. Anyone vote against going? No? Then it's decided."

"Do you really vote on stuff?" Mark asked as they went to Scott's room.

"A lot of times. And no one gets their way if they're the only one for or against."

"Not even if it's your dad?"

"No, I can't remember if that ever happened."

"At my house, it's what Dad says that goes. Like Mom didn't really want to go on this trip. But Dad said she should, so she did. He decided."

"She did decide in a way. She decided to do what your dad said."

"I guess so."

"You been to the place we're going before?" Mark asked as they walked toward the car.

"Sure. I like it and know some stories about it. The Shawnee Indians there used to send smoke signals that some one picked up and sent on as far as Cincinnati."

Scott told other stories as they rode first on one state road and then turned onto another. "The settlers used the canal to ship things, then the railroads came and put the Whitewater Canal out of business."

"Then why is Metamora there?"

"Because someone wanted to keep it as it was. They call it restoring. They aren't allowed to have modern stuff like neon signs there."

"There won't be many people here today and not all the places are open during the week," Liz Hardesty said as Scott's father parked the car. "The Canal House will be and some others like the Candy and Candle Shop. But I'd rather come now than on weekends. It's too crowded then."

"Come on, Mark," Scott said. "Let's see if the canal boat is running. Yes! I see the horses waiting on the bank. See you, Mom. Shall we meet you here?"

"Yes. After your ride, we'll go eat."

The boys were the only ones on the flat-roofed boat for several minutes. The man who took their tickets said, "We'll wait for a few more passengers. There's a couple of busloads of people here somewheres. One's from Covington, Kentucky, and one from a place called Winchester. I don't know in what state."

The boys looked over both sides of the boat and took a seat at the front. "That way we won't have ladies on both sides of us," Mark said.

"You won't have any on either side," Scott said. He was glad to be seated before anyone else boarded. *There's no use to have people looking at this poor little lame kid,* he thought.

When the boat began to glide, Mark couldn't sit still. He acted as if he wanted to look in all directions at the same time. "See how the water parts ahead. And there's a bridge up there. Will we go on *top* of it?"

"Yes, there's sort of a channel in it. I forget

how many inches deep. The boat will make the water spill over into the river below. It'll make a rushing sound like a bridge-long waterfall."

"Where does it go?"

"Into the Whitewater River below. Way down. Those are the locks up there. They used to lift boats up and down. We won't go through them. They don't work anymore."

"Then how will we get back?"

"That's easy. They hitch the horse to the other end of the boat and we go the other way."

"I'd like to take another ride," Mark said. "If your folks don't care."

"They won't. We can go again after we eat."

"We'll eat in the Root Beer Cellar. Not many other places are open," Liz Hardesty said when they joined her. She led the way down curving steps to a long room with walls of the same kind of stone as the steps. Bottles of colored glass with light bulbs inside were the wall lamps. Wire-backed chairs were placed around small round tables. As they ate cheese sandwiches and fat pretzels with mugs of foamy root beer, Mark talked about the canal boat and asked questions about the town of Metamora.

"We need to start home by three o'clock," Scott's father said as they went up to the vine-shaded patio. "Here, wear my watch, son."

"I have one," Mark said, "but it runs too fast. It gains a lot."

The boys watched water run under the giant

wheel of the mill where grain was ground and saw a man knead a mound of chocolate fudge into long rolls. They bought a quarter pound between them and had it divided into an even number of pieces.

As Scott's father turned the ignition key, Mark took a deep breath. "This is really a super great place. And just think, I didn't even know about it until today."

Liz Hardesty turned sideways in the front seat and said, "I often think that there are a lot of *super great* places for us to discover. And thousands of books for us to read, and all sorts of things waiting for us."

"I know what's waiting for us tomorrow," Mark said. "And a bunch of other days."

"You mean school?" Scott's mother said. "Don't you like it?"

"Well, not all of it."

"He says recess is his favorite subject," Scott said.

"I know it's not a subject," Mark said, "but it's the best thing at school. I'm good at what I do then."

"That brings up an interesting question," Scott's father said. "Are we good at what we do best because we like it, or do we like it because that's what we do best?"

"That's sort of complicated, Dad."

"I know. That's why I've never come up with an answer."

60

Scott didn't talk until they were within sight of home. He thought about the things they'd done while in the canal town. *The boat rides were best. They always are. But another thing's great. Seeing good things fixed up like they used to be, made better. Is it the same with a boy's leg maybe?*

8

THE BOYS didn't sleep in the lighthouse that night. There were two TV shows they wanted to watch and by that time they were sleepy and didn't choose to climb the ladder. When morning came, Mark hurried to his home on his bike after breakfast. "I need to feed stuff and take in the mail before today's comes."

"Are you coming back?"

"I was thinking I might not today. I mean, the bus comes at one. I might take a bath and change into my clean clothes. Then I couldn't do much playing."

"You'd better talk to my mom. We're supposed to be taking care of you."

Liz Hardesty listened and said, "I see your

point. If you change your mind, we'll be here. But how about lunch?"

"I can heat something in the microwave. Mom lets me."

After Mark left Scott walked to the front porch and sat sideways in the slatted porch swing, with his legs stretched toward the other end. One leg reached farther than the other. *If I have that operation and the tendon does stretch, maybe both of them will touch the other arm,* he thought.

"Feeling lonely?" his mother asked from the other side of the screen door.

"No, not really. Mom, did you ever get tired of having someone with you?" He hadn't meant to ask the question. It slipped out.

"Certainly. There comes a time for visits to end."

"But it's not time," Scott said. "Mark's dad and mom aren't back."

"I know. But that's probably why he chose to be at home for a few hours. He needs to be alone."

"It makes me feel a little ashamed to be glad he's gone."

"Disloyal perhaps? I don't think you need to feel guilty," Scott's mother said. "You've crowded a lot of activity into these last two days and nights. We all need a rest once in awhile, a time of quietness."

"Some kids don't—like those who live in New

Burlington," Scott said. "They're together all the time."

"I know. But I think they still need quiet times. Too much togetherness is wearing. Trying to think up things to do sometimes gets them in trouble."

Scott had changed into school clothes and was eating a toasted cheese sandwich when the telephone rang. "I'll get it. Hello."

"Scott," Mark said, "something's changed. When I got home my grandma and grandpa from up at the lake were here. Could I ask your mom something?"

"Sure. Hold on."

Scott listened, but his mother didn't say much. Just things like "I see" and "That's true" and "I'll tell him. I'm sure Jenny would approve."

"He's going to stay with them?" Scott asked when his mother turned from the phone.

"Well, to be more exact, they're going to stay with him," his mother said. "Mark told me he'd see you on the bus. Or would you rather I took you to school?"

"No, the bus is okay." As Scott went to his room he thought, *Some things aren't good on the bus, at least not sometimes. But if I sit up front I don't hear so much junky talk, and I don't end up in the middle of the hitting.*

He pushed the button on the aquarium light and counted to ten, giving the milky tube time to flicker, then glow. He reached for a can of flaked fish food. *I think they know it's me, the way they swim around in circles. Or could be they're just super-hungry.*

He waited on the front porch until he saw the bus leave Mark's house. *I'll have time to be out there waiting. The kids won't have to see me hump-thumping along, if they're looking.*

"Hey there, young man," Mr. Middleton said. "Are you ready and raring to get another year's education?"

"I guess so. There's not much choice," Scott said. "Is it okay if I sit here?"

"Sure is. If I'd put names on the seats yours would be in gold letters." As he sat down Scott thought, *Where's Mark? He's usually sitting here.*

"Your partner waved me on," Mr. Middleton said. "Someone must be taking him."

"Probably." Scott didn't try to talk to the driver while they were moving. *He's always looking back and front and both ways to make sure nothing is coming,* Scott thought. *I don't want to bother him.*

Scott walked toward the school alone when the bus had unloaded. Some kids said "Hi" as they passed him. No one slowed down. *That's okay. Last year at this time I was in a wheelchair and couldn't start school. So this year is better—a lot better."*

He knew he'd been assigned to Mrs. Hudson's room. *That was good news,* he thought. *She came*

65

to see me and brought books when she wasn't even my teacher. I wish Mark was in the same room. But we've been separated before. It didn't make any difference then. Even when I was absent, he kept on being my friend.

The first session only lasted an hour and a half. Mrs. Hudson gave out lists of supplies they'd need—notebook and paper, pencil, ruler, and something called a protractor. "You'll pick up your rental books tomorrow, when the fees are paid," she told them.

As Scott left his room, Mark caught up with him. "You're lucky."

"I am?"

"Sure, you got Mrs. Hudson. Me, I got old Grouch-face. Besides, Raymie's in my room. Double trouble."

"Who's Miss Grouch-face? I never heard *that?*"

"Oh, she's new. That's what some kids called her."

It didn't take long for kids to name her, Scott thought. *That's not very fair.*

"I'm going someplace with my grandpa. I don't know where. See you."

Scott's mother was pouring lemonade into three tall glasses when he walked into the kitchen. He knew she'd had them in the freezer. Otherwise they'd not be so frosty. He asked, "Why three?"

"Your father's coming from his shower. The wheat's all sown."

66

"Are we having a meeting?" Scott asked. "You always put oatmeal cookies out when we are. At least it seems like you do."

"Well, as a matter of fact we are," his mother said. "We can't really put this one off any longer."

Scott's throat felt tight. *I know what it's about. I just know.*

John Hardesty came out, buttoning the cuffs of his blue shirt after he sat down across the table from Scott.

Scott wanted to say, "I know what you're going to talk about. The operation." But the words wouldn't come.

"Dr. White called this afternoon," his mother said. "I went in to talk to him and find out more about the operation. I've taken notes and will explain what I heard, as much as I can."

Scott listened, but didn't look up. He kept his eyes on the frosty glass. *She's not saying much that's new. I heard before about slitting the short tendon and putting a piece into it to stretch it.*

"Does Doc think this should be done now?"

"Not necessarily. Since it's been over a year, a few more months won't make that much difference. He suggested that you go to the hospital the day after Christmas. That way you won't have to miss so much school."

"Some way to spend vacation," John Hardesty said as he thumped his doubled fist on the table.

"I know," Scott's mother agreed.

67

"Can they be sure this operation will help?" Scott's father asked.

"Yes, it will help. How much they can't tell."

"You mean my legs will be nearer the same length?" Scott asked.

"Yes, your heel will not be pulled up. Not as much, anyway. How do *you* feel about this, Scott?"

"I don't know. Not for sure. Being better's not as good as being the same as I was. But it'd still be better. Right?"

"That's the way I feel," his mother said. "Well, we don't have to decide right now. But I think we should be grateful there's some help available, and that there's a leg to be mended."

"Meanwhile," Scott's father said, "what's this I hear about you playing ball? And practicing in the barn? Why didn't you talk about this?"

Scott felt a little embarrassed. He shook his head. "I don't know. Maybe I just had to see if I could be any good."

"I felt sure you would be," his mother said. "With all that thumping."

"What do you mean. Did you—"

"Did I know what you were doing? Listen, mothers *do* catch on. Did I know why? I could only guess."

"Guess what?"

"That you didn't like being the last one chosen."

"How did you know—"

68

"Scott Hardesty! I've been there. I was scared if a ball came toward me. I'd even shut my eyes. No wonder no one ever wanted me on their side. A batter with her eyes shut doesn't have a good hitting average."

"If you'd said something, I'd have pitched to you," Scott's father said. "I'm not too bad."

"Could you hit a knothole eight times out of twelve?"

"I might. If you let me stand close enough."

9

SCOTT didn't see Mark until they went to school on Tuesday morning. The Labor Day weekend had been filled with family activity. A trip to the shopping center in Muncie, a picnic along the east side of the reservoir, and Sunday morning church services. There hadn't been much time for Scott to think about the operation he might have. *But sometimes it pops into my mind,* he thought as he waited for the bus on the first full day of school.

He watched a squirrel scamper across the grass and up the trunk of a maple tree. *It's probably been out looking for something to eat,* he thought. *But not like our breakfast. They eat whenever they find something, if they're hungry.*

I wonder who invented meals? And who decided we'd have three meals a day? How do such things come to be?

Mark took a deep breath after he took the seat beside Scott on the bus. "Well, here we go, ready or not."

"Ready or not for what?"

"For a whole year of school."

Maybe for you, Scott thought. *I might be stuck in the hospital part of the time.* He wanted to tell Mark that he might be having an operation. *But that would sound like I want him to feel sorry for me. He'll find out if—*

"You mad at me for something?"

"Why would I be mad at you? What made you think that?"

"Well, you aren't talking much," Mark said.

"Oh, I was just thinking about why I'm not upset about school. Maybe it's because I had to miss a lot last year or—"

"Or what?"

"Nothing. Maybe nothing," Scott said.

"Anyway, here we go, ready or not. But I still wish we could be in the same room."

"Me too," Scott said. He didn't see any need to say that sometimes it might be good that they weren't always on the playground at the same time—just for part of the noon hour. *This way Mark won't feel like he has to choose me when it's his turn to pick sides. He might now that he knows about me pitching at the knothole.*

Scott didn't think about baseballs or operations or even about being lame until after lunch. Mrs. Hudson talked for nearly half an hour about a new thing called *special projects*. "Each one will choose a subject and work on it alone. I'll consult with each of you once a week and will help you find materials if that's what you need."

She answered more than a dozen questions, most of them being, "What can I do?" Scott didn't hold up his hand. He didn't have any questions. He didn't need anyone to help him decide on a topic. "I'd like to know more about lots of things. But there's one main thing. Tropical fish."

He'd saved almost enough money to buy another aquarium and he'd thought of trying to raise angelfish. *They'd be okay by themselves, where they couldn't hurt other fish. I could keep a notebook and draw pictures or paste some in.* Then he remembered the hospital. *Would Mom take care of them while I go—if I do? She probably would.*

Raymie bumped into Scott as they left the cafeteria. "Let me around, will you?" he said. "I got to get out there or I won't get to pitch."

"You're already around," Scott said, but Raymie was too far away to hear.

Scott blinked as he walked into the bright sunshine. Voices came from all over the playground. "It's kind of like music, some high, some not, but not too great."

A ball game had started. *Raymie didn't get to*

pitch, Scott noticed. *He's sitting over there on the grass—probably mad.* Scott walked to the walnut tree along the fence and sat down, leaning against the trunk. *I'm not exactly hiding. But I'd sooner Mark didn't see me, didn't try to get me to play. Kids would say all kinds of stuff if I went thump-bumping around the bases.*

He felt lonely, more left out than he had for awhile. *I guess Mark didn't even look to see if I'm here.*

Someone tall came from the direction of the school. A long shadow danced on the grass. "Need an extra playground supervisor?" Mrs. Hudson asked.

"That's not what *I* am. That's you today, huh?"

"Yes. I drew first duty," Mrs. Hudson said. "Would you object if I sit with you?"

"No. Why?"

"Oh, Scott, you know kids. Being friendly with teachers isn't—what do they call it? Cool?"

"Sometimes they say cool. Sometimes it's *tough*. But they don't bother me much. I've been called worse."

"You have—why? Or perhaps I shouldn't ask."

"It's okay. Because of my foot is the main thing."

"Oh, Scott. That's cruel."

All at once Scott knew he was going to tell his teacher about the operation. "It might be better for me some day," he told her. "Not all the way good, but better though."

Mrs. Hudson listened while he explained that the shortened tendon would be slit, then stretched some way. She asked questions. Some Scott could answer, some he couldn't.

"Do you dread being in the hospital again?"

Scott nodded as he ran one finger up and down on the back of his other hand. "Yeah. But in some ways it's not going to be as bad as before. One thing, my leg's not all torn up like then. So I might not be in the hospital as long. But it'll still hurt. Besides, I've already missed a lot of school."

"Don't worry about that," Mrs. Hudson said. "There'll be no problem. I'll stop by once in a while and give you your assignments. There'd probably not be many days when you'd not feel like working."

"Probably not. But that would sure take a lot of your time wouldn't it?"

"Not *too* much."

"Would someone pay you? My dad and mother?"

"Not your parents, and I'm not sure you'd be out long enough to qualify for homebound tutoring. But that's not important. We'll take care of the lessons. Besides, I owe someone."

"Owe?"

"Yes. I was out of school for a long time, nearly a year, when I was younger than you. I had something which doctors would probably call *rheumatic fever* now. A neighbor, a retired teacher, helped me keep up. She said she needed to be needed. I never could repay her. She moved away two years later. Well, I'd better get on my feet. The bell will be clanging in a minute or two."

Scott stood up, wiggling the leg that had been hurt. It went to sleep sometimes if he stayed in one position. As the bell rang, Mark came running past and then stopped so suddenly that his red baseball cap fell to the grass. "I didn't see you over here. Why didn't you come around?"

Scott shrugged his shoulders. "I didn't want to be in the way. Who won?"

"*They* did, Mr. Trent came over and made us let old Raymie pitch part time. That's why we got beat. The other team got three runs from Raymie Run-on."

Scott laughed. "That's a little funny. Three runs off Raymie Run-on."

"Not to me," Mark said. "It's not one bit funny."

As Mark left and went down the hall Scott thought, *Raymie's not the only one who calls people names. Mark does it to him and to his teacher. I guess I do too sometimes.*

The fifth graders in Mrs. Hudson's class were leafing through their social studies workbooks when Mr. Trent came into the room. As he talked with the other teacher, Scott watched them. *Mrs. Hudson's not happy about whatever he's saying,* Scott thought. *Her face has pink spots and she's twisting her ring round and round.*

"I'm sorry to interrupt you at your work," the

teacher said. "Mr. Trent has something to say."

"I've talked to our principal," Mr. Trent said. He glanced at Mrs. Hudson before going on. He's given me permission to organize noon leagues. Everyone will play. Sports should be for all of you."

Scott looked down at the open workbook. *Now the fun's gone out of noon recess for me. I'll be scared when it's my time to be on someone's team. No one will want me, unless it's Mark. And he might not if I make a mess of things.*

Before he took the cap from the ballpoint pen he thought, *Anyway if I go to the hospital, I can't play then. But that'll be winter time when no one can play.*

10

WHEN SCOTT'S mother called him the next morning he thought she'd made a mistake, looked at the clock wrong or something. *It's not near daylight,* he thought as he raised up on one elbow and looked toward the window. *No wonder it's dark. It's raining—hard. And that's thunder.* He yawned and stretched his arms back over his head, grasping a brass pole in each hand. *It seems like my arms are getting stronger. Maybe it's because I've exercised like this a lot. Or it could be from throwing that ball at the knothole.*

As he dressed for school a new thought came to his mind. *It seems sort of funny. I did all that throwing so I wouldn't be the last one chosen. Now I'm not wanting to be picked to be on any noon league team. That's funny all right—"funny peculiar," as Dad says.*

His father was standing at the back door when Scott walked into the kitchen. "This is a real turkey drowner," he said.

"I never heard you say that before," Scott said. "You mean the water's deep enough to drown an old tom?"

"No, not that," John Hardesty said. "Sometimes turkeys stand around in the rain with their heads up and actually drown."

"That's dumb," Scott said.

"Perhaps that's why we call a person who's not too smart a turkey sometimes."

As Scott poured maple syrup over three triangles of French toast he thought of other things his father said over and over. *Do they make sense to him, like about the turkey, even if they don't to me? Like when he says there are more trees in the woods than anyplace else, and everything's connected to everything.*

"I don't know what I'll do with myself today if this downpour keeps up," Scott's father said.

"I can think of a few jobs," Liz Hardesty said, "as I've told you before time and again."

"No doubt. No doubt."

"So can I, Dad," Scott said. "Only I guess I'd better tell you more, to see if it's okay and everything." He explained about the special school project and his idea of learning more about tropical fish.

78

"Sounds good," his father said. "I have no objections, but how does this involve me?"

"Well," Scott said. "I have enough money, almost anyway, for another aquarium. And I'd need something to put it on. There's not enough room on that old chest of drawers."

"Well, let me think about this. I'll do some measuring and we'll talk more after school. I might even make a trip to a lumberyard."

"I'd better ask Mrs. Hudson if this is an okay project," Scott said. "But I think she'll say yes." Then Scott remembered what his teacher had said about tutoring. *I'd better tell them. But I don't really want to bring up the subject. I'm not in any hurry for that operation. Besides, the bus would be here before I'd get it all said.*

Scott was busy all morning at school. He didn't even go out for first recess. His conference with the teacher about his special project ran over the fifteen minutes each person was allowed. She approved of the theme and offered to send to the state library for books with color illustrations.

"I'd like to see your fish," she said. "If I come to help you, I can. Did you—"

"You mean did I talk to Mom and Dad about you wanting to help me? No, but I will when the operation's a sure thing. And I think it will be."

As Scott slid his tray along the pair of poles in front of the serving counter in the cafeteria, he thought, *I wouldn't care if I had to stay in at noon. Why did that old Mr. Trent think he could decide what everyone should do? After all, it is a recess—not a gym class. That's bad enough! Now this.*

He ate slowly. No one noticed that he stayed at the table after the second group of classes came for lunch. He thought of going back for seconds on milk. He had some money left. *But I'm not really hungry.*

When Scott reached the playground, Mr. Trent was blowing a whistle. *Looks like he'd run out of wind. Not many kids are paying any attention to him,* Scott thought. *Just the ones who usually play ball.* He decided that if others were getting out of being in the noon games he'd try walking away. As he turned around he heard Mark yell, "I take Hardesty."

For the first time he felt angry at his friend. *I'm almost all the way mad, not just a little mad like when he tries to boss me when no one's around. This is different. He's putting me on the spot in front of everyone.* As he walked to the left side of the grassless diamond he heard someone say, "What can *he* do?"

After the sides were chosen, one team had twelve players, the other thirteen. "We'll let it go," Mr. Trent said. "There won't be time to play everyone. Some of you will have to sit out for a while."

Good, Scott thought. *That might let me out.* He sat down on the backless bench and watched the game as the other team took the field. He glanced

80

at the sky and saw that a jet plane had left a wavy vapor trail in the pale blue sky. *What makes it wavy? A little wind? Or isn't something working right?*

Lonnie Glenn pitched for Mark's side. *He's okay*, Scott thought. *I won't get put in to bat for him. He can hit better than most guys who pitch.* As Scott's team came up to bat he was thinking about what would happen to the kids who didn't come when Mr. Trent whistled. Suddenly the teacher reached past two other players and pointed at Scott. "You pinch hit for Glenn," he said. "Mark says you have a good eye."

But not too good a leg, Scott thought. As Scott walked across the dusty ground he heard someone on the other team say, "Here's an easy out—a piece of cake, you guys."

Scott's ears felt as hot as if he'd stood with the bat over his shoulder long enough for them to be sunburned. *Old Mark's going to feel sorry he ever picked me. He might not want to be my friend if I let him down now. I guess I ought to try.*

He purposely didn't swing at the first ball. He hadn't been watching the pitcher. *I'll watch now, and see how the ball comes toward me.* He didn't feel upset when the math teacher-umpire yelled, "Strike." It was a strike—not too high, too low, nor outside.

He swung hard at the next pitch. He missed but heard the bat and the ball pass one another. *The whish of air sounded like in the barn when balls bounced back past me, after I got so I could throw harder,* Scott thought.

Scott felt sure that he'd hit the next pitch. *It's like I got a signal or something.* He didn't think about the yelling. He swung. The crack of the bat on the ball was sharp and clear. He dropped the bat and was on the way to first base before the other players had time to begin to yell. He didn't look to see that the ball was still in the air until after he'd headed toward second. Then he saw it begin to sink far beyond center field, as far as the fence or farther. He knew he could make it home. *Even if my running is about like other people's walking, I'll get there.*

Mark ran out to meet him, thumped his shoulders, and said, "I guess you showed 'em, Scott. Here, I'll let you wear my cap."

Scott grinned and said, "You keep it. You're up next." He knew that Mark had bought the cap in Cincinnati and had worn it for two years. His mom said he'd sleep in it if he wasn't afraid of breaking the bill.

"Where'd you learn to hit like that, Hardesty?" Mr. Trent asked. "Did you play a lot before you were hurt?"

"No, not much. Baseball wasn't my thing."

"Then how did you get so good?"

Scott felt sure that he'd hit the third pitch. "It's like I got a signal or something." He didn't think about the yelling.

"Oh, I practiced when I didn't have anything else to do." Scott didn't want to tell Mr. Trent about the knothole. He didn't want the others to hear about that either. *Besides, I don't know myself how I did it. Not for sure. I'm glad I made a home run. But Mark's more excited than I am.*

Raymie came up to Scott after the bell rang. "You sure got lucky, Hardesty. Not many get a break like that, especially not a—"

"Stop right there, Raymie," Mark said. "Whatever you were going to say, don't. Now listen good. Shut up."

11

SCOTT didn't talk much on the way home, but Mark did. "You could get to be a pinch hitter, a regular one, if you keep on practicing. As long as you can slam a bat like that."

"Maybe," Scott said. He thought of telling Mark that the new operation on his leg was almost a sure thing. *But I don't want other kids to hear. And with his high hopes for me, he might feel let down.*

As he walked from the road to the house he thought about his own feelings. *As much as I practiced, it seems like I'd be the one to be excited. Someone chose me to be on their team. And I did okay. But for me it's not so great to play as it is for Mark. Did I think it would be? I can't re-*

member if I ever pictured playing. I just worried about not being picked.*

He looked toward the open doors of the garage. *The car's here, but not Dad's truck. He could be back in the field or in the woods. He planned to cut some firewood for the stove he ordered.*

Scott stopped inside the kitchen door and listened. He heard a humming sound and knew his mother was sewing. "I'm home," he called.

"Come on up. After you rummage for a snack."

There's not much rummaging to do, Scott thought. *She left chunks of cheese and apple slices in plain sight.*

"Where's Dad?" Scott asked when he reached the top of the stairs. "Cutting wood?"

"No. He was going to price lumber in case Mrs. Hudson okays your project. And then he said he might stop by the Farmer's Auction."

"Why? Is he going to buy something?"

"I doubt it," Scott's mother said. "He rarely does."

"He goes to talk to people, right?"

"Partly. And to see how much things are selling for. Did you have a good day?"

"Yes," Scott said as he sat down in the low rocker by the double windows in the small room. "For one thing, I hit a home run. It went so far I made it around all the bases. I had plenty of time. I could have made it by walking even, instead of trotting."

"How did that make you feel?" his mother

asked as she clipped loose threads from the seam she'd stitched.

"Sort of surprised. But Mark was real excited. He yelled, and jumped up and down, and pounded my back."

"I wish I could have seen that," his mother said. "And your dad."

"I don't think Dad would have wanted to be there."

"Why—what makes you say a thing like that?"

" 'Cause I still limped. He watches me walk and looks sad a lot of times."

"Oh, Scott. You're not thinking that your father's *ashamed* of you?"

"Well—he could be. I mean, he played basketball and he's real strong."

Liz Hardesty pushed the straight chair back from the sewing machine table, walked over to Scott, and knelt down beside him. "Your dad is pained because your one leg is shorter. But surely you know why he feels that way."

"You mean he thinks he should have kept me from being hurt?"

"Oh, yes. You think of him as being strong. And he is in most ways. But he's been shaken by sobs many nights."

"I didn't know that."

"He didn't want you to see him."

Scott saw the tears in his mother's eyes. *Are they for Dad, or me, or all of us?*

"You think Dad still hurts about my leg?"

"Yes, he does. Not as much. Time heals, and you've helped by working hard to regain the strength in your leg."

"Well, Mom, it's not that bad to me. I mean I do about everything I want to do. I'm not as fast as before, but I get there. Hey, look out the window. What's Dad got in the truck? It's something bright orange, but I can't see much of it over the sideboards."

His mother pulled the curtain away from the glass. "It's a riding mower or a garden tractor. I can't tell which."

"I guess he bought something at the sale this time. I'm going to see if he'll let me ride this one."

"Wait! Tie your shoes. Don't break a leg over a shoe string."

As the screen door banged behind Scott, his father was leaning the second heavy plank against the open end of the pickup truck. "Looks like you bought a tractor," Scott said.

His father scratched his chin and acted as if he was puzzled. "Is that what this is? I've been trying to decide all the way home what this piece of machinery was. I didn't want to expose my ignorance by asking in front of half the people of Perry Township."

"Could I learn to drive it, Dad?" Scott asked. "I'd be careful and do what you tell me to do."

The smile that Scott had seen on his father's face was gone all at once, like it melted.

"Why don't we talk this over as we eat?" Scott's

mother said from the yard gate.

"That's a good idea," John Hardesty said. "I have to put out hay for the cows first. Want to ride along, either of you?"

"If you are to eat, I'll need to stay here and finish getting it ready," Scott's mother said.

"And I've not finished the chores on my work chart," Scott said. As he emptied the waste-baskets into plastic bags and filled the woodbox for the fireplace, he thought of how it would be if he could drive the riding mower. *If I get good enough and show Dad I can be careful, I might get jobs mowing yards. Greg probably won't want to keep on mowing Mrs. Hudson's cause he's a carry-out boy. This way I could pay her back for helping me with my lessons, if I have the operation—which I probably will.*

"It's colder, Mom," he said as he went to the bathroom to scrub up for supper.

"Sometimes it turns cold this early in September. But we'll still have warm days. And Indian summer comes after the first frost."

"Why do they call it Indian summer?" Scott asked.

"I don't know. I've never gone to the bother of looking up the answer."

"Could we have a fire tonight? It's been a long time," Scott said.

"I don't know why not. If you'll take over and finish setting the table for me, I'll light one. Then it'll be down to glowing coals by the time we've eaten. If I do a good job, maybe you could find some marshmallows in the freezer and put them out to thaw."

As they ate hamburger pie which was dotted with mashed potato pillows, Scott's mother said, "Tell your father about your home run."

"You hit a home run? In a ball game?"

"Sure," Scott said. "I was a pinch hitter and on the third pitch something happened. It was like I couldn't miss the ball. It went so far—way over the fence—I had lots of time to get home."

"Do you think you'll keep playing?"

"I don't know. I mean it was real great to be chosen. Mark was the one who picked me. I'd have felt terrible if I'd struck out—on account of Mark partly. But it's not like I thought it would be."

"Can you tell us what you mean?" his mother asked.

"Well, it's like being chosen is not so important now that I have been—anyway not for baseball. It's not my favorite thing. Maybe I'll like it better if I could choose what is special for me, I mean."

Scott's father reached across the table. "I want to shake your hand."

"You do? Why?"

"Why? Well, I'll tell you. I've lived twenty-three years longer than you have, and I never realized something before. It's better to choose than to be chosen. That's a powerful thought."

Dad's proud of me. And not because of the

*home run or because I made it around the bases.
It's like my short leg doesn't make any difference
anymore—at least not as much.*

"What's for dessert, Liz?"

"Apple pie—either with cheese or ice cream."

"Could it wait until later?"

"Well, yes—but why? Did you forget to feed
something?"

"No, but it will soon be dark and I have a lesson
to give. Come on, Scott. You did ask if you could
learn to drive the mower? Am I right?"

"You certainly are."

As Scott reached for his jacket his mother came
to him and hugged him. He saw tears shining in
her eyes. He didn't have to ask why. These were
good tears, not like the sad ones he'd seen when
they talked in the sewing room.

"Wow," he said as he hurried to the kitchen
door. "Just wait until I tell Mark about this."

12

BY THE TIME the light in the barn lot flickered into a milky glow Scott had learned to start the riding mower, shift the gears, and regulate the speed. He made three trips down the lane, across the grass, then up and across to the lane without his dad on the back. "Tomorrow we'll practice letting the mower blade down. Now it's pie time."

Scott felt trembly as he walked to the house. *It's like the shaking and the roaring of the motor is going on inside me.*

"You two scrub and see if you can get rid of the gasoline smell," Scott's mother said. "I don't want that to spoil my buttery cinnamoned apple pie."

"Yummy! *Buttery cinnamoned*, that sounds good," Scott said.

They took the plates of dessert to the family room and watched television as they ate. When the hour-long program was over Scott's father said, "Let's turn this off for awhile."

"I know what's coming," Scott thought. *"That business about the operation."*

When his father began to talk he decided he'd been wrong. "I priced lumber for your project, Scott, in case it's approved. And I cam up with this idea. Would it spoil your fun if we put the new aquarium in this room? That way all of us can enjoy watching the fish."

"I approve," Scott's mother said. "I find myself stopping in your room to watch them. They have a calming effect on me."

"Me too," Scott said. "Sometimes I leave the light on. All the rest of the room's dark. I get real sleepy but then I wake myself getting up to turn off the light. Twice I didn't and left it on all night."

"You didn't say, Scott. Would you like to share your project with us?"

"Sure. I didn't think about you liking them that much. Besides, if I have the operation I'd be down here for awhile." He looked at his feet. *Why did I say that? I didn't want to talk about that. Now I mentioned it myself.*

"Are you ready to talk about the operation?" Scott's mother asked.

"Might as well. I'm getting tired of trying not to talk about it."

"I think we've all wished we could postpone this decision," his mother said.

"I've talked to Dr. White twice lately," Scott's father said.

"Are you sick or something?" Scott asked.

"No, nothing like that. I had questions about your operation and needed some answers."

"Did you get them?"

"Yes, there's no doubt that the operation will help. You probably will still limp, but not so much."

"And we'd never forgive ourselves if we didn't give you this chance," Liz Hardesty said. "We're like you—we see you getting along well. And we hate to put you through a painful time. We hurt when you do."

"That's what Raymie says his dad tells him when he beats him," Scott said.

"Beats him?"

"That's what Raymie calls it. He says his dad tells him that the strap hurts him worse than Raymie. That's dumb."

"Do you suppose he abuses that boy?" Liz asked.

"I wouldn't be surprised," Scott's father said. "I've seen him yank on the bridle of that riding horse of his until the bit brought blood."

"But Raymie's his son."

"Cruelty is cruelty," John Hardesty said.

"Does Raymie sound—well, angry—at his father?" Scott's mother asked.

"No, not exactly," Scott said. "But I don't think he likes him much. He calls him the old man and other stuff. I guess he's used to whatever his dad does."

"Well, I'm going to be on the watch for bruises."

"Be careful, Liz," Scott's father said. "You could get in trouble, poking into family matters."

"Not now. The law's changed. We're in trouble if we don't report child abuse."

Scott wished he hadn't said anything about the beatings. *I'd really be in trouble if Mom reports something and Raymie got mad. Or would he be glad?*

"Let's get back to our situation," John Hardesty said. "Should we give the doctor the go ahead sign? Any nos?"

Scott wanted to hold up his hand, part of him did. *But it wouldn't be right not to do what Doctor White thinks is best, and what would make Mom and Dad feel better.*

"Now that we've settled that matter, where should we put the aquarium table?" They decided on the corner away from any windows.

"Too much sun makes green algae grow," Scott said.

"And by putting it there it would be in our line of sight when we're seated to watch television."

"That's right, Mom. We can rest our eyes by

95

switching from the news to guppies and from mysteries to mollies."

Scott's father measured and wrote figures on a small pad. "Mrs. Hudson said she'd help me with my lessons," Scott said.

"You talked to her about this already?"

"Yes. I didn't mean to. It sort of slipped out."

"Have you said anything to Mark?"

"No, but I don't know why."

Scott's mother put her arm around his shoulders. "Are you worried how Mark will act? That he might change?"

"I guess. He might get tired of waiting on me to be more like other kids."

"Has he said anything to make you feel this way?"

"No," Scott said. "Only I know he's going to try to get me to play ball. I sort of wish I hadn't hit that home run. But I did learn something."

"What's that?"

"That baseball's sort of boring for me. Just that one day I couldn't keep my mind on the game. I watched a jet vapor trail and a couple of tumble bugs."

"Exercise is important," his mother said.

"I know, but Mark and I don't have to do the same things. I like to swim. But I don't want to beat anyone—just swim."

"Nothing wrong with that," his father said. "Now we've been serious long enough for one night. How'd you like to take a ride?"

"It's already after eight," Liz said. "And—"

"And tomorrow's a school day, Mom. We *know.*"

"We won't be gone long," his dad said. "I'm in the mood for a game of miniature golf. It won't be long until it's too cold to play."

Dad knows I like miniature golf, Scott thought as he walked to the car. *He knows I can keep up okay. I'm not sure how much he likes the game himself.*

"Want to ask Mark?" Scott's mother said as she shut the door of the car. "We can stop by."

"No, not this time. It's okay with just us."

They played two games before Liz Hardesty said, "It's time to go. Each of you have won a game. I wouldn't win if we played all night, and I'd prefer not to live with either of you if you won two."

"Do you get the idea she doesn't like competition?" Scott's father asked.

"That's probably why I don't—partly anyway," Scott said.

They bought Dairy Dream cones, two butterscotch and one strawberry yogurt, and ate them on the way home. Scott felt good. *I don't know why. It's decided about the operation, but things are better for me than some people. Like Raymie. I wouldn't want to be in his shoes, even if his legs are both the same length.*

As Scott followed his mother through the gate, he saw the moon above the trees in the east woods. *It's more gold than silver tonight. It looks bigger than it does a lot of times. I wonder why? It's still the same moon. I'll have to find that out—like a lot of other things.*

13

MARK began talking about baseball as soon as he sat down beside Scott on the bus the next morning. "It's really super good, I mean with the noon leagues. I can hardly wait. I'll pick you every time—if I'm the one who gets to choose."

"Don't worry about leaving me out," Scott said. "I'd just as soon you would."

"That's a dumb thing for you to say."

"So, I'm dumb."

Scott turned and looked out the bus window. *It's like we're standing still and the telephone poles and fence posts are going the other way.*

"I didn't mean *dumb* dumb," Mark said. "You know that—I mean you get a lot better grades than I do in most things."

"It's okay."

"You're mad," Mark said. "I can tell. When you say it's okay and don't look at me, I know it's not."

The bus pulled up to the walk. Scott waited until Mark and most of the other riders went out the door. He walked alone. *I think Mark's the one who's mad. Or maybe he's just tired of walking with a slowpoke like me.*

"Hey, wait a minute Scott," someone called from the water fountain.

He turned and saw Davie Landon coming toward him. *I don't think it's Danny, because this twin is a little fatter than the other.*

"You got your special project picked out?" Davie asked.

"I think so. Mrs. Hudson says it's okay, and I'm sure it's something I like. It's tropical fish. What's yours?"

"Mine's sort of different for a boy. It's about cooking—how recipes can be changed and still be good. I like to experiment."

"Is Danny doing a project too? The same one?"

"No. His room's not into this. Anyway, he wouldn't. We're not *that* much alike."

"You're together a lot," Scott said as they went to their seats.

"I know, but not like before. Not since we can't be in the same room."

"Do you like that way better?"

"It's okay. I'm used to being on my own. Dan—

well he's the leader—sort of bossy sometimes. Hey, I forgot what I meant to say, the main thing. That home run you hit really surprised me."

"Me too," Scott said.

"Do you think you'll get to play today?" Davie asked.

"I hope not."

"Why do you say that?" Davie asked. "I thought you'd be really keen about getting another chance after you did so good."

"Well, I'm not. I wanted to be chosen, sure. But playing's not—well I just don't like it that much."

"Me neither. I don't think we ought to *have* to do anything at noon."

"Well, Mr. Trent thinks so."

"I know."

Mrs. Hudson was calling the roll when a voice came over the loud speaker. "Good morning, Sutton School students. This is your principal." Scott listened to the announcements about the Brownie meeting after school and book rental money being due Friday. "We are dropping the idea of having organized leagues at noon. This project was put into effect without proper consideration."

Scott looked across the aisle. Davie was smiling and shaking hands with himself. *That's a relief,* Scott thought. *But a lot of kids like Mark will play anyway. I probably won't see much of him. It won't make much difference to him now if I miss a lot of school.*

Scott sat with the Landon twins at noon. He didn't see Mark until he was taking his tray to the racks outside the kitchen. "I guess you heard about our fun being spoiled," Mark said.

"Not mine. Besides, you can still play, if that's what you want."

"Are you still mad?" Mark asked.

"No, but you probably still think I'm dumb."

"I *said* I didn't."

Okay," Scott said. "Forget it. See you on the bus." As Mark grabbed his ball glove from the end of the table Scott thought, *He didn't even hear what I said. He was thinking about playing ball.*

Danny Landon followed Mark but Davie went with Scott. They walked to the edge of the school yard and looked over the fence. They watched some of the workmen who were helping to build the new middle school. "They sure have to know a lot," Davie said, "how to put up the steel beams or whatever you call them, and bricks and other stuff."

"Not everyone knows it all," Scott said. "My dad's on the school board. Different bunches of people do different things, like the wiring and the cement work and the bricklaying."

"We'll be going there year after next."

"I know."

"Does the idea of going to a new school scare you?"

"No, not much. But it would if I had to go to

102

another town. Something else scares me now though." He hadn't planned to tell Davie, but he found himself talking about the operation. *With Mark I've kept from saying something about it. Why didn't I now?*

Davie listened and didn't ask any questions until Scott said, "That's how it is."

"I'd be scared too. But if you'll be better, then it's okay. Right?"

"As right as it can be. I can do most things I want now. Then I'll probably be able to do more."

"Like what?"

"Oh, I can't think of anything right now. Maybe later I will."

Mark sat down by Scott on the bus and they talked. *But not much,* Scott thought. *It's like there's too much we don't want to say to each other. Will we ever be close friends again? Probably, part of the time, anyway.*

His father was walking away from the mailbox at the side of the road when Scott stepped from the bus. "Hi, Dad."

"Hi to you. Did you have a good day?"

"It was okay. Is Mom home?"

"No, she went to the shopping center. How'd you like to mow the yard? Hopefully this is the last time it'll need it this fall."

"Not hopefully for me."

After the mower had clipped the grass, after many square turns, Scott and his father sat on the back step. They enjoyed the ginger cookies

and fruit punch which had been left on the table. "You know something, Scott," his father said. "I think the time's come when I can tell you how much I approve of you."

"You do?"

"I do. Notice I didn't say *proud*. Saying that would mean I had something to do with what I approve of. Does that make sense?"

"In a way. But I didn't think you—"

"Didn't think I what?"

Scott's throat felt so tight it hurt. "That you were proud of me—not like the other dads could be. Because I'm sort of crippled."

Scott felt his father's arm across his shoulders. "I should have faced this before. But I was a coward."

"You *were?*"

"Yes. I had all this pain because of my part in what happened that day. I couldn't face up. But it wasn't you that shamed me. It was my own feelings."

Scott looked up and saw tears in his father's eyes. "Don't feel bad, Dad. You told me to stay back from the mower. I forgot how far it reached when I grabbed for Sport."

"But it's what you've done since, the way you've gone on, that gives me a better feeling

Scott was glad his father asked him to mow the lawn. His father hoped it was the last time this fall, but Scott hoped it wasn't.

about it all. You've shown a lot of courage. Like your mom says over and over, we're a lucky bunch of people."

Dad, is three a *bunch?*"

"Sure, the Hardesty bunch. Now, it's time for me to haul corn to the hogs."

"Could I ride with you on the tractor?"

His father rubbed his hand over Scott's hair. "Sure. Why not? Change your clothes first."

As Scott went up the stairs he listened again to the sound his feet made. Before reaching for his patched jeans he walked to the aquarium and pressed the button on the hood. Red swordfish, black mollies, fan-tailed guppies, and orange platys swam in darting circles.

"You know me don't you?" Scott said. "You heard me coming. Some of these days you won't know it's me. My feet won't sound the same. You'll have to get used to me all over again. So will I."

Gary Burney photo

Dorothy Hamilton, a homemaker from Selma, Indiana, began writing books after she became a grandmother. As a private tutor, she has helped hundreds of students with learning difficulties. Many of her books reflect the hurts she observed in her students. She offers hope to others in similar circumstances.

Mindy is caught in the middle of her parents' divorce. *Charco* and his family live on unemployment checks. *Jason* would like to attend a trade school but his parents want him to go to college.

Other titles include: *Amanda Fair* (shoplifting), *Anita's Choice* (migrant workers), *Bittersweet Days* (snobbery at school), *The Blue Caboose* (less expensive housing), *Busboys at Big Bend* (Mexican-American friendship), *The Castle* (friendship), *Christmas for Holly* and *Holly's New Year* (a foster child), *Cricket* (a pony story), *Eric's Discovery* (vandalism), *The Gift of a Home* (problems of becoming rich), and *Gina In-Between* (accepting her widowed mother's boyfriend).

Mrs. Hamilton is also author of *Last One Chosen* (a handicapped boy), *Jim Musco* (a Delaware Indian boy), *Ken's Hideout* (his father died), *Kerry* (growing up), *Linda's Rain Tree* (a black girl), *Mari's Mountain* (a runaway girl), *Neva's Patchwork Pillow* (Appalachia), *Rosalie* and *Rosalie at Eleven* (life in Grandma's day), *Scamp and the Blizzard Boys* (friendship in a winter storm), *Straight Mark* (drugs), *Tony Savala* (a Basque boy), and *Winter Girl* (jealousy).

Four books of adult fiction by Mrs. Hamilton are also available: *Settled Furrows* and a trilogy on family relationships—*The Killdeer*, *The Quail*, and *The Eagle*.

In addition to writing, Mrs. Hamilton has spoken to more than 300,000 students in five states, Canada, and 48 counties of Indiana.

"What's your favorite part in writing a book?" one young student asked.

"Right now, it's being here with you," she replied.

"The prospect of facing 80 fifth- and sixth-graders at the same time is enough to send many adults for the nearest exit," a news reporter noted, "but for Dorothy Hamilton it is pure delight."